Original title:

Branches and Ballads

Copyright © 2025 Creative Arts Management OÜ

All rights reserved.

Author: Maxwell Donovan

ISBN HARDBACK: 978-1-80566-751-3

ISBN PAPERBACK: 978-1-80566-821-3

Stanzas Born from the Earth's Heart

In the woods, a squirrel jives,
Doing the twist while the tree trunk thrives.
Acorns dance in the breeze with glee,
Who knew a nut could throw such a spree?

A raccoon sings to the stars at night,
Wearing a mask, oh what a sight!
He steals from the pantry, thinks he's suave,
But his dance moves are truly a farce.

Mushrooms giggle at the tales they weave,
Each story wilder than we believe.
They party till dawn with the muddy ground,
In nature's fest, laughter knows no bound.

An owl hoots, a wide-eyed friend,
Singing to echoes that never end.
With wisdom and jokes, he rules the night,
But in daylight, he's a sleepy sight.

Verses from the Mossy Mounds

In the shade of mossy heaps,
A squirrel danced while the rabbit leaps.
They giggled at the fawning fawn,
As the sun set, they played till dawn.

The mushrooms looked like tiny hats,
As frogs sang tunes to nearby sprats.
One snorted loud, 'That's quite the beat!'
While ants in line found a jolly treat.

The Harmony of Hidden Trails

Amidst the green and winding paths,
The raccoons plotted their silly wraths.
With pail hats made of hollowed nuts,
They danced and twirled with little butts.

The owls hooted from the lofty trees,
Sipping nectar from the buzzing bees.
'Is this a march or just a stroll?'
Chirped the crickets with a comedic roll.

Odes to the Stalwart Pines

The pines stood tall with a regal air,
While squirrels chattered without a care.
'Knock knock!' one yelled from his tree house,
'Who's there?' cried out a surprised mouse.

The branches nodded, living in glee,
As pinecones tumbled 'round merrily.
'Let's hold a party! Bring your own snack!'
They laughed and twirled, never looking back.

Refrains in the Ambrosial Air

With a breeze that tickled the leaves,
Bees buzzed tunes that no one believes.
They swayed in rhythm, rather absurd,
Creating laughter unheard, unheard!

The chorus sang by the rippling brook,
Even fishes joined in, shaking a hook.
'We're a band!' they cheered with delight,
In this silly world, all felt just right.

The Chorus of Climbing Vines

In the jungle, vines do prance,
Swinging low, they take a chance.
They tell tales of clumsy flies,
And laugh at cats with silly sighs.

A sloth joins in, swings a bit wide,
With rhythm that can't quite abide.
The parrot squawks, 'Let's give a cheer!'
Yet everyone just points and sneers.

Harmony in the Hushed Understory.

Underneath the leafy dome,
Squirrels chatter, feel at home.
With acorns dropped like clumsy notes,
And melodies from singing goats.

A frog croaks loud, it's quite a show,
While worms just wiggle, 'Go! Go! Go!'
The owl hoots laughter up above,
As everyone forgets the love.

Whispers of Twisting Vines

The twisting paths where laughter winds,
Are tangled tales that fate unwinds.
A raccoon tugs at laces loose,
While ants dance on, with all their juice.

A breeze slips by, a playful ghost,
It flicks the leaves, which giggle most.
Amidst the fun, a snail did jest,
'What's the rush? I like my rest!'

Song of the Wind's Embrace

The wind sings soft through leafy trails,
It tells of fish with furry tails.
A lizard jigs, a rabbit hops,
While bees provide the pulsing pops.

The breeze makes everyone feel bold,
Except for those too shy and cold.
Sway to the rhythm, take a chance,
And join the dance, oh sweet romance!

Sagas of the Verdant Vistas

In the shade where the squirrels play,
The acorns dance and bounce all day.
A hedgehog sings in a crooked tune,
While raccoons applaud beneath the moon.

A wise old owl with spectacles,
Claims to know the forest's tentacles.
But trip on roots and branches he will,
And tumble down with a fateful thrill.

Ballads from Below the Canopy

The chipmunks chatter with chirpy glee,
While mischievous ants march in a spree.
A skunk with flair dons a top hat tight,
Proclaims he's the star of the forest night.

With mushrooms as seats, the critters gather,
To hear a tale of the big tree's bladder.
It's rumored its roots can tickle and tease,
And make the toughest of critters sneeze!

Songs of the Twisted Trunks

A twisted tree told a rhyming jest,
Of branches that stretch but never rest.
With a wink and a sway, he swirled around,
Where laughter echoed, a fun place found.

The badger crooned with a voice so sweet,
About a raccoon who lost his seat.
He rolled and tumbled, a jolly show,
While the trees chuckled, putting on a glow.

Whispers of the Woodland Wisp

A wisp of light with a giggly grin,
Darted around like it's chasing kin.
It tickled the toes of foxes at play,
Who barked with laughter, 'Hey, come this way!'

The trees leaned closer, their gossip swayed,
"Did you hear what the owl claimed?"
"Oh, do tell us, oh where is the fun?"
"A dance-off with frogs has just begun!"

Echoes of the Forest Floor

Upon the ground where critters play,
A squirrel with nuts, he lost today.
He jumped and spun, what a silly sight,
With every leap, he lost his bite.

The ants parade like tiny trucks,
While beetles dance, oh what a fuss!
They spin around in acrobatic glee,
Mocking all who come to see.

A bunny hops, with style and flair,
Chasing shadows, without a care.
With every turn, he trips a bit,
Laughing loud, he won't admit.

Down by the brook, fish splash with joy,
A tangle of weeds, oh what a ploy!
They tease the frogs who croak and croon,
A concert near, beneath the moon.

Melodies of the Verdant Vault

In the canopy, a crow sings bold,
His notes are twisted, a sight to behold.
He flaps and hops on a branch, oh dear,
Chasing his echo, not quite sincere.

A raccoon waltzes on the edge of dusk,
Snatching snacks, he's quite the musk.
His masked face hides a grin so wide,
As he juggles treats on a daring ride.

The wind whispers secrets to all nearby,
Tickling the leaves as they wave goodbye.
With a giggle, the whispers start,
Making even the toughest heart.

Under the boughs, they gather around,
With laughter and joy, no frown can be found.
Each note and chuckle blends in the air,
A symphony of fun, beyond compare.

The Dance of Leaves and Lyrics

Oh swirling leaves in a playful breeze,
They twirl and dip, like dancers with ease.
A caterpillar joins in the fun,
With a shimmy and shake, he thinks he's the one.

The chittering sparrows create some sass,
With chirps and twitters, they frolic en masse.
A couple of them steal the show,
Strutting like stars in a bright tableau.

A fallen twig becomes a stage,
For ants to act their tiny age.
With tiny reigns, they ride on a shoe,
What a charade, a hilarious view!

At twilight's edge, the laughter grows,
As critters mingle in their own prose.
Every flick of a tail, every squeak and sound,
Turns the forest floor to a carnival ground.

Serenades of the Sunlit Glade

In the bright glade where sunbeams play,
A shy lizard performs, come see his sway.
With wiggly moves and a flick of the tail,
He charms the bugs without fail.

A group of frogs form a croaky choir,
Their loud harmonies will surely inspire.
With each note, they leap and dive,
Creating ripples, feeling so alive.

Beneath the shade, a turtle hums,
To the rhythm of buzzing, oh how it drums.
He dreams of racing but takes it slow,
While dragonflies steal the lightning show.

As dusk blankets the glade with cheer,
The critters gather, drawing near.
With laughter echoing in the fading light,
They celebrate the day, what a delight!

Harmonies of Bark and Bloom

In the garden, trees whisper, oh so loud,
Squirrels gossip, gathering their crowd.
A raccoon tap-dances, quite the show,
While the flowerpot tries to steal the glow.

Bees hum serenades of sticky delight,
While daisies wear sunglasses, looking bright.
A caterpillar croons, dreaming of flight,
As the wind plays piano through the night.

The sun winks down, a playful tease,
As branches giggle in the gentle breeze.
A shadow prances, soft yet bold,
While the worms spin tales of treasure untold.

In every nook, a song takes its start,
Nature's orchestra plays from the heart.
So join the dance, let your laughter bloom,
In this whimsical world where joy finds room.

Melodies of Swaying Limbs

The branches sway like dancers on a spree,
While the grass rolls its eyes, 'Oh, let it be!'
The moon chuckles, dressed in silver sheen,
As the bushes gossip, feeling quite keen.

A woodpecker knocks, a cheerful beat,
Making tunes from the old oak seat.
The frogs croak harmony, all in a row,
While the fireflies twinkle, putting on a show.

The wind joins in with a playful sigh,
As squirrels launch acorns, oh my, oh my!
Every limb has a story to share,
In this backyard, laughter fills the air.

Nature's choir sings, all night long,
With crickets strumming a bassline strong.
So grab a seat and join in the fun,
Where each note is a blessing under the sun.

Chants of the Woodland Spirits

In the forest, giggles echo like chimes,
As sprites poke fun at the ancient rhymes.
A gopher performs in a top hat grand,
Turning up the charm, just as he planned.

The trees bend low to catch every jest,
While mushrooms debate who wears the best vest.
A fox sings a ballad, tail in a whirl,
While critters join in, giving life a twirl.

Stumps host a party, with fairies galore,
As the owls hoot, wanting nothing more.
The fog rolls in, crafting a veil so neat,
Distracting the beetles who dance on their feet.

With echoes of laughter, the night takes flight,
In the heart of the woods, under stars so bright.
So follow the trail where the shadows sway,
And let the woodland spirits lead the way.

Verse of the Rooted Souls

In the garden of giggles, where roots intertwine,
Laughter sprouts up like a well-timed line.
The daisies declare a silly revolution,
While the toadstools cheer in joyful contribution.

At dawn, the broccoli wears a crown of dew,
While carrots compete in a dance or two.
The potatoes roll on the ground, oh so bold,
Sharing stories of adventures untold.

Each leaf is a storyteller, drifting along,
Crafting verses in nature's whimsical song.
The sun beams down, tickling all it can find,
While garden gnomes laugh, not falling behind.

So come take a stroll, let your heart feel whole,
Among the cheeky blooms, and the rooted souls.
For in this patch, joy's a natural goal,
Where the funny and the friendly make magic in whole.

Melodic Dances of the willowy Savior

In the forest, they groove and sway,
Savior of laughter, come what may.
Twisting and twirling with joyful cheer,
Whispers of mischief hang in the air.

Under boughs where shadows play,
They trip and tumble, what a display!
Jigs to the rhythm of birds up high,
A symphony crafted beneath the sky.

Laughter echoes from leaf to leaf,
Bouncing melodies, a dance of relief.
Swaying to tunes that tickle the leaves,
Each shuffle and wiggle, the forest believes!

Watch those limbs stretch and bend,
As humor and harmony cleverly blend.
In nature's embrace, they find their call,
The melodic dances, enchanting us all.

Elegy of the Silvered Saplings

Oh, the young ones, dressed in silver sheen,
Moping about like they're part of a scene.
Whispering woes to a passing breeze,
"What about us? We need some expertise!"

An old oak chuckles, cracks a wide grin,
"Life's a giggle, let the fun begin!
With roots below and humor above,
Remember dear saplings, that laughter's the love."

Each leaf joins in, shimmying about,
Creating a chorus, there's no doubt!
In the shade of giants, they sing and sway,
An elegy bright, for a merry ballet.

Oh little ones, in glistening rows,
Forget your sorrows, let joy compose!
With every silvered leaf that twitters,
A symphony brewed from giggles and flitters.

Treble of the Forest Floor

On the forest floor, a tune so spry,
Mushrooms are dancing, oh me, oh my!
With toadstools tapping in rowdy delight,
They form a chorus under soft moonlight.

Squirrels join in with a cheeky cheer,
Chasing their shadows, no sign of fear.
Their antics amusing, a merry parade,
Frolicking freely, giving joy an upgrade!

The melody rises, soft rustles abound,
Each chuckle and chortle, a whimsical sound.
An orchestra formed of nature's own crew,
Making a ruckus—how lively they grew!

From roots to the sky, the spirit is pure,
With laughter as fuel, every heart can endure.
Treble notes play on, as night turns to dawn,
In a concert of joy, forever reborn.

Riffs from Nature's Palette

Nature's musicians play wild and free,
Strumming the strings of the elder tree.
With branches like fingers, they pluck at the air,
Creating a symphony without any care.

Fluffy clouds drift by in joyous refrain,
While buzzards above join in the campaign.
A riff full of quirks, each note has its place,
The woodland serenade, a funky embrace.

Grasses sway gently, keeping the time,
While crickets and frogs jump into the rhyme.
A jam session crafted by leaves all around,
In the heart of the forest, pure laughter resounds.

From petals to bark, the beauty is clear,
Each note that is played brings the world some cheer.
So let's dance along to this playful ballet,
Where riffs of the wild invite joy every day!

The Chorus of the Nature's Theatre

In the woods where laughter rings,
Frogs are crooning, flapping wings.
Squirrels tap dance on the boughs,
While grasshoppers take their bows.

Breezes whisk away the tunes,
As chipmunks hum beneath the moons.
Critters gather for a show,
With costumes made of leaves that glow.

Shimmering Notes in Dappled Sunlight

Sunbeams play on leaves so bright,
Bees buzz by, a funny sight.
A rabbit starts to breakdance there,
While butterflies twirl in the air.

The sun's applause lights up the scene,
Caterpillars join the routine.
They wiggle, giggle, do their best,
To invite the flowers to the fest.

Whispered Lyrics on Gentle Streams

Rippling waters softly hum,
Fish are flopping, look so dumb!
A heron's trying to keep cool,
While ducks parade, they act like fools.

Each wave brings a silly rhyme,
As turtles play their tricks on time.
The breeze reminds them not to pout,
Nature sings, all's fun, no doubt.

The Harmony of Life Unseen

Behind the trees, the critters play,
As raccoons roll in bright hay.
They chuckle at the passing breeze,
And plot to steal some honeybees.

The owls hoot, a comic host,
As fireflies dance, they brag and boast.
In nature's symphony so grand,
The laughter echoes over the land.

Echoes in the Canopy

Beneath the sky, the critters dance,
A squirrel's twist, a daring prance.
With acorn hats, they take the lead,
In laughing loops, they plant their seed.

The birds in tune, they chirp so bright,
A woodpecker joins, a comical sight.
They joke of nuts and stolen seeds,
While shadows stretch, fulfilling needs.

The breeze it whispers, a playful tease,
Tickling leaves with mischievous ease.
As sunlight filters through the hues,
They clap their wings and share their blues.

A bounce of branches, their laughter spun,
As twilight falls, their fun's begun.
In laughter's echo, they find their glee,
In this grand canopy, wild and free.

Serenade of Leafy Shadows

In tangled shades, the whispers hum,
A frog leaps high, a wacky drum.
The snails in shell suits, marching slow,
Regale the crowd with their grand show.

The owls throw darts of funny quips,
While crickets chirp their funky scripts.
Beneath the cloak of leafy sway,
They jest and jive till the end of the day.

Their laughter rings as the dusk draws nigh,
A raccoon winks with a sly, sly eye.
In moonlit chaos, they dance, they shout,
In leafy shadows, it's all about clout.

With jars of fireflies, they start to glow,
Creating tunes that ebb and flow.
In this serenade, joy knows no end,
In shadows they frolic, and wits they blend.

Rhythms Beneath the Boughs

Underneath the leafy shade,
The rabbits joke as they parade.
With floppy ears and silly hops,
They stage their acts and never stop.

Each rustling leaf, a tap for fun,
A mouse joins in, 'Oh, what a run!'
They spin and tumble, a comical sight,
As laughter erupts in the fading light.

The winds play tunes, a jazzy flair,
As chipmunks giggle without a care.
In merry rhythms, they swing along,
Belting out their offbeat song.

With tree trunks as props, they climb so high,
Balancing dreams with a silly sigh.
Together they weave, with joy and sound,
In this vibrant dance, true magic is found.

Lullabies of the Forest Treetops

A raccoon sings of moonlit nights,
With catchy tunes, to our delight.
The owls join in, a gentle croon,
Lulling the stars, their nighttime swoon.

As shadows swirl in playful guise,
The night critters share their wise alibis.
A hedgehog strums a tiny guitar,
While everyone dreams of travel far.

The breeze it dances with whispered tales,
Of silly scrapes and wobbly trails.
Each note a tickle, each rhyme a kiss,
In treetop lullabies, it's pure bliss.

When morning breaks with a playful yawn,
The sleepyheads stretch, their stories drawn.
In this forest choir, joy takes flight,
With laugh-filled dreams that sparkle bright.

Crooning of the Sunlit Dell

In the dell where squirrels dance,
The sunlight gives a silly glance.
A rabbit hops with cheeky glee,
As butterflies hum harmoniously.

The daisies jiggle, light as air,
While dandelions toss their hair.
A frog joins in with a croak so bold,
As if he's wearing a crown of gold.

The sunbeams tickle every petal,
While giggling flowers form a kettle.
The breeze is laughing, weaving tales,
Of silly singsong and happy trails.

In the end, the day must rest,
While critters share their funniest jest.
They clink their cups of dew-filled cheer,
In the dell, we laugh and steer.

The Story of Wind-Kissed Leaves

Whispers tickle every leaf,
In the breeze, there's no belief.
Leaves argue about their fall,
One claiming it has no recall.

A squirrel giggles in the trees,
Dropping acorns like they're fees.
The leaves all flutter in delight,
As laughter takes to flight at night.

They wag their tips in playful glee,
Sparks of mischief, wild as can be.
A gust comes by, they twirl and sway,
In a waltz that steals the day.

With every gust, a new tale spins,
Of tumbling down and cheeky wins.
The ground receives their jolly cheer,
For laughter's never far, my dear.

Resonance of Time-Worn Trunks

Weathered trunks with stories old,
Crackling laughter like a mold.
They share secrets with the breeze,
Of countless dreams beneath their leaves.

A woodpecker knocks a tune,
While shadows dance beneath the moon.
Each knot and groove, a giggle caught,
Of all the silly battles fought.

The trunks remember tales of yore,
Of squirrel thieves and items galore.
A porcupine tells jokes so sweet,
While ants march by with tiny feet.

In twilight's glow, they snicker low,
Reviving tales that ebb and flow.
With every year, their humor grows,
In laughter's grasp, the forest glows.

Yearning for Forest's Return

When autumn whispers in the air,
A pine sighs loud, "Are we still here?"
It craves the laughs of yesteryears,
   Longing for joy that disappears.

The mushrooms chuckle, standing proud,
In funny hats, they're feeling loud.
They remember the fun, the crazy times,
   When every day wrote silly rhymes.

The ferns all nod with wavy glee,
"I miss the squirrels, come back to me!"
The forest echoes with quirks galore,
   As nostalgia knocks on every door.

Let laughter rain, let the fun return,
For nature's heart still has a yearn.
In every nook, in every glen,
   The spirit of joy will bloom again.

The Saga of the Old Growth

In a forest thick and round,
Old tree trunks stand their ground.
With whispers of the past, they tease,
About the squirrels and their cheese.

Each branch has tales that twist and bend,
Of mushrooms that they called friend.
Leaves laugh as the breezes blow,
Sharing secrets of the crow.

Mossy hats atop their heads,
They gossip near their leafy beds.
Their stories all begin with luck,
Of a lost sock and a hungry duck.

So if you stroll that wooded way,
Just stop and listen, hold your sway.
For laughter hides where shadows play,
In ancient tales of the heyday.

Twilight Verses in the Thicket

As dusk descends in leafy glades,
The critters dance in light escalades.
Frogs croak tunes with deft delight,
While fireflies twinkle, oh what a sight!

There's a raccoon, king of the crew,
With a disco ball made just for two.
His partner, a beaver with snazzy moves,
Together they glide as the night improves.

A chorus of owls hoot in glee,
Their wisdom shared in harmony.
One owl jokes, "Who's there to roast?
Just me and these nuts, let's have a toast!"

So dance through thickets, don't you stall,
Where laughter echoes, we're having a ball.
Nature's twinkling, grand finale,
In twilight's glow, the funny rally.

Unfurling Stories of Green Canvases

On verdant stages, tales unfold,
Of prickly pears that boast so bold.
A turtle once tried to race the snail,
But ended up in a leafy frail.

Chasing shadows, a badger trips,
While a fox stands firm with wobbly hips.
A parade of ants in perfect sync,
They march on sprouts and start to wink.

Bumblebees buzz, but not in fright,
They hum the tunes of a berry fight.
With nectar plucked, they weave their song,
In a garden where silliness belongs.

So wander through this green, wide space,
Where stories bloom and laughter's grace.
With every rustle, a new delight,
In nature's art, it's pure starlight.

The Music of Azure Skies

Under skies of bright azure hue,
A cheeky parrot sings just for you.
With flapping wings and a silly dance,
He'll twirl on air in a feathered trance.

Clouds become marshmallows overhead,
As the sun yells, "Onward!" having fed.
A gathering of pigeons, stylish and neat,
Debate about flying and the best route to beat.

The laughable breeze, it nudges the trees,
Tickling leaves with a gentle tease.
A squirrel chimes in, "Don't lose your way!
Follow the giggles, that's where we'll play."

So lift your spirits, let's soar and glide,
On heavenly notes, let joy be your guide.
In the symphony of the sky so grand,
You'll find the fun, just take my hand.

Acorns of the Echoing Past

Underneath the ancient oak,
Squirrels plot their heist with glee.
Each acorn's worth a golden joke,
As they dance around the tree.

Rusty leaves start to proclaim,
"Catch me if you can, oh fool!"
Nature plays her funny game,
We're all the actors in her school.

A whisper stirs the hollow bark,
Old spirits giggle in the night.
A chain of laughter starts to spark,
Echoing in pure delight.

So let's be merry, let us sing,
The acorns chuckle, the branches sway.
Life's a stage, and we're the fling,
Living silly in our own ballet.

Threnody of the Enduring Thorns

Amidst the brambles, there's a tune,
A prickle-fest of joy and pain.
Each thorn holds secrets by the moon,
Which leaves us grinning through the rain.

The rosebud laughs at its own plight,
"Look at me! I'm sweet and fierce!"
While bumblebees buzz in delight,
Dancing while the thorns do pierce.

We sing a dirge but can't resist,
The weirdness of this thorny plight.
With every snag, comes a twist,
In this odd dance of day and night.

So here's to thorns that make us yell,
A prickly path to laughter's goal.
In the tangle of the wittiest swell,
We find our joy, we find our soul.

The Secret Symphony of Wilderness

In whispering woods, the frogs conduct,
A crazy choir of ribbits loud.
Symphonic chaos, nature's pluck,
While crickets chirp and sing aloud.

A rabbit hops to the wacky beat,
Mice join in with their tiny steps.
The trees sway, their rhythm neat,
As if nature's up to some wild preps.

The maestro owl hoots with pride,
As raccoons clap in the twilight.
Through tangled vines and shadows wide,
The wilderness roars with delight.

So let the wild ones strum their strings,
In this amusing moonlit show.
Join the folly, as laughter rings,
In this secret place we all know.

Nocturne of the Shadows Cast

When daylight fades, the jokes begin,
Shadows twist and giggle 'round.
With every flicker, it's a win,
As they dance without a sound.

A cat that pounces on the night,
Turns into a jester, sly.
With every slip, a pure delight,
The moon just winks and rolls on by.

Laughter floats on gentle breeze,
As unknown pranksters take their shot.
The darkness teases, plays with ease,
In this absurd, funny plot.

So here's to shadows that delight,
And moonlit pranks that make us laugh.
In the night's caress, all's alright,
Life's serious side feels the gaff.

Symphony of Twigs and Melodies

In a forest where laughter sings,
Twigs play tunes on butterfly wings,
Squirrels dance in a crazy spin,
Chirping birds all join in the din.

Frogs croak out with much delight,
While raccoons choreograph a night,
Laughter echoes, leaves do sway,
Nature's band in wild display.

A chipmunk solo, oh what a sight,
Singing loud with all its might,
While the hedgehogs hum along,
In this chaos, we all belong.

As branches sway in playful glee,
Creating a show for all to see,
Nature's humor, wild and free,
Tickling hearts, a jubilee.

Lament of the Sunlit Glade

In a glade where shadows play,
The sun trips on its golden ray,
A squirrel tries to catch its beam,
While frogs croak out a silly dream.

Golden rays slip through the leaves,
Tickled by the playful eaves,
Each beam a jester, bright and bold,
Entertaining stories told.

The bumblebee buzzes a tune,
Interrupting the moth's hot noon,
While daisies gossip, swaying neat,
Sharing tales of their sunny feet.

Then all at once a shadow cast,
A bird missteps, it didn't last,
And as it flutters, laughter flows,
In this glade where sunshine glows.

Notes Among the Foliage

Leaves gossip breezy secrets loud,
As ants form up a marching crowd,
The flowers shake their heads and sigh,
At clumsy beetles zooming by.

Each rustle carries quirky tunes,
From leaping frogs that croon at moons,
A squirrel's scurry makes a beat,
That echoes joy beneath our feet.

The wind, it howls a merry song,
As petals dance and twirls along,
Nature's chorus fills the air,
With giggles spun, it casts a flare.

So gather close, and hear the cheer,
For nature's music always near,
In every branch, and every leaf,
A playful verse beyond belief.

Cadence of Flora's Heart

In the meadow, flowers sway,
Singing songs of bright ballet,
A daisy twirls, with merry flair,
While tulips giggle without a care.

The breezes tickle, laughter swells,
As every leaf a story tells,
A bumblebee buzzes the beat,
In this rhythm, we find our seat.

Petals toss in cheeky glee,
While crickets step out joyfully,
The sun beams down with a wink,
As weeds and roses start to sync.

When twilight falls, the tunes don't stop,
As crickets chirp and flowers hop,
In this garden where joy imparts,
We dance along, with flora's heart.

Echoing Melodies of the Grove

In the thicket, where critters prance,
A squirrel stole a glance, did a little dance.
The wind whispered jokes, oh what a sight,
As leaves chuckled softly, tickling the night.

A raccoon played a tune on a hollow log,
While frogs croaked rhythms, jumping like a fog.
The moon played piano, casting its beams,
And fireflies twinkled, igniting our dreams.

An owl hooted puns, wisdom-filled delight,
While shadows danced silly, in the pale starlight.
Laughter echoed through an enchanted glen,
As nature's own jesters performed once again.

So if you wander under twilight's care,
Listen for laughter, it's floating in air.
For every tree is a storyteller bold,
In this comical grove where secrets unfold.

The Lyricist's Labelled Leaves

In the library of whispers, the leaves were a page,
Each flutter a lyric, each twist a sage.
Caterpillars giggled, drafting their dreams,
While spiders spun verses in silken esteem.

A leaf lost its label, and oh what a fuss,
It tried on new names, like Fuzzy or Gust.
The branches held gossip, they cackled with cheer,
As the breeze spread the tales far and near.

The sunlight penned ballads with warm, golden ink,
While shadows grew clever and started to think.
With notes of confusion, they made a delight,
A symphony written in giggles of light.

So next time you stroll 'neath the leafy embrace,
Remember the laughter that dwells in this space.
For every green story has humor indeed,
In the pages of nature, let joy be your creed.

Serenade of the Swaying Sidelines

On the edge of the meadow, the grasses sway,
With a cheeky little wink, they invite you to play.
The dandelions danced with a sunny flair,
As giggles erupted from nooks everywhere.

A butterfly argued with a buzzing bee,
About who was better at tickling a tree.
With laughter as petals, they twirled in delight,
Making ruckus in hues, oh, what a sight!

The stones chimed in with a clattering cheer,
Reciting great tales from yesteryear.
With whispers of mischief in every soft gust,
The edges of nature turn giggles to dust.

So join in the chorus of playful refrain,
Let laughter lead you through sunshine and rain.
For in every corner where nature takes lead,
There's humor and melody, that's all that you need.

Memoirs of the Noble Foliage

In the court of the woods, where trees wear their crowns,
Stories are traded in quirky sounds.
A wise old trunk told of a fumble and slip,
When a bird lost its way on a clumsy trip.

The leaves shared their secrets, so curious and spry,
Of squirrels who plotted, yet never flew high.
With branches as pens, they scribbled with fun,
Creating a saga 'til the setting sun.

The roots chuckled deep in the rich, loamy earth,
Organizing pranks since the moment of birth.
With echoes of laughter that twist in the breeze,
Every whispering limb grants a mirthful tease.

So wander these memoirs of nature's parade,
Where hilarity thrives in light and in shade.
For every tall story begins with a grin,
In the fertile domain where life spins and spins.

Whispers of the Canopy

In the green heights, a squirrel gabs,
Chasing dreams of acorn jabs.
Leaves giggle when they sway,
As branches play hide and seek all day.

The sun tickles with its beam,
While birds plot their feathery scheme.
A dance of shadows lick the ground,
Where laughter of nature can be found.

A wise old owl hoots a jest,
About a cabbage dressed as a vest.
The clouds roll in with heavy sighs,
While raindrops play hopscotch from the skies.

In this arboreal fiesta grand,
Life is funny, not just planned.
With giggles echoing through the leaves,
Nature's humor, the heart believes.

Songs of the Wind's Embrace

The wind sings songs both silly and gay,
As pinecones dance and twirl away.
A gust whispers secrets to the trees,
While acorns chuckle, floating on the breeze.

A parrot yells, 'I'm a flying stew!',
While hummingbirds strut, in vibrant hue.
Crickets compose a night-time ball,
As moonlight shines on nature's hall.

With every gust, a new playful tune,
As frogs croak loudly beneath the moon.
The owls join in with their quirky hoots,
Making melodies from leafy roots.

Underneath this starry dome,
Every creature feels at home.
Their laughter blends with the soft night air,
In a concert of joy, beyond compare.

Tales Woven in Twigs

Once a twig had dreams to soar,
To be a wand or maybe more.
A beetle tips his tiny hat,
And said, 'You'll never be a cat!'

The robins tell of love-struck ants,
Who dance with grace in leaf-strewn pants.
A tale of lizards playing tag,
While the ladybugs all boast and brag.

In a knot of ivy, stories grow,
Of foxes who tap dance in a row.
Each twist and turn a giggle spins,
In the chronicles of woodland wins.

For every story, a chuckle awaits,
As squirrels steal from nature's plates.
In the realm of twigs and tales,
Every creature in laughter prevails.

Harmonies Beneath the Boughs

Beneath the trees, a raucous sound,
As critters gather 'round the ground.
A raccoon whispers, 'What's that smell?'
While singing mice weave a funny spell.

They strum on mushrooms, a wild tune,
While ants march in, a lively platoon.
The slugs glide slow, with grace they roam,
Making sure they're never alone.

A botanist dreams of a plant ballet,
While bees buzz by, like sweet cabaret.
Every leaf seems to join the cheer,
In this hilarious woodland sphere.

So when you wander through the trees,
Listen closely, if you please.
For laughter blooms where nature's found,
In the heart of the leafy ground.

Lullabies of the Twilight Grove

In the twilight wood, critters chat,
A squirrel in shades, wearing a hat.
The owls gossip, full of cheer,
While raccoons juggle snacks so dear.

The frogs croak tunes of delight,
As fireflies dance, oh what a sight!
Bunnies tap their tiny feet,
A merry ruckus, can't be beat.

A deer hums low with a grin,
While mushrooms giggle, tucked within.
The breeze whispers secrets near,
As twilight hums, let's grab a beer!

The moon's a smile, wide and bright,
Lifting spirits into the night.
In this grove, laughter is free,
Discover joy under each tree.

The Songbird's Serenade at Dusk

Birds with flair, perched on a wire,
Chirping tales of clownish attire.
A parrot tries rapping, oh what a sound,
While the crow shows off pranks, round and round.

The goldfinch winks, dressed so fine,
And the sparrow claims each song is divine.
With a twist and a hop, they perform with zest,
Their evening concert, you'd think it was blessed.

A puffball puffs up to lead the show,
While crickets break out in a toe-tapping row.
Under the twilight, this scene so surreal,
Funny moments, a delightful deal.

As night blankets all, they surely will brag,
About the fun times, no notes they will bag.
Who knew that soft tunes could spin such a tale,
With laughter and joy, they will never fail.

Cantatas of the Rustic Realm

In fields of green, the cows all hum,
Telling jokes with each silly thrum.
Goats play the drums, a band on the rise,
While pigs do the moonwalk, oh what a surprise!

The farmer laughs at their jiving spree,
As chickens shake wings, what a sight to see!
With each purr and cluck, the night takes flight,
Creating a concert that feels just right.

Mice bring the cheese for a savory tune,
As owls spin stories under the moon.
This ensemble of critters, a whimsical sight,
Turns the mundane into sheer delight.

So gather 'round for this rustic blast,
Where fun never fades, and laughter will last.
In this realm, where nature's the star,
Each melody shines, no matter how bizarre.

Stanzas of the Gnarled Old Oak

A gnarled oak sat with wisdom so deep,
Telling tales that would make you leap.
With branches that twisted in puzzling ways,
It chuckled with mirth in sunshine and haze.

Critters gather 'round for their daily dose,
Of comedy wrapped in the bark of prose.
Squirrels play tag, dodging the breeze,
While raccoons hold court, masters of tease.

With each rustle of leaves, laughter erupts,
As the old oak supports all of their setups.
From acorns to antics, the fun never wanes,
These stories of life keep turning the reins.

As morning peeks through the leafy embrace,
The oak shares its humor with charming grace.
And under its boughs, life dances and spins,
A timeless ballad where joy always wins.

The Serenade of Fluttering Wings

A chicken danced atop the fence,
Singing songs that made no sense.
The rooster joined with great delight,
But flapped too hard and took a flight.

The ducks quacked loud, a listening crew,
As a squirrel played the kazoo.
They laughed at notes both sharp and flat,
As the old dog dreamt and chased a cat.

A butterfly with style so nifty,
Joined this party all quite shifty.
With wobbly wings, it took a spin,
And landed right on the turkey's chin.

So gather round for this feathered spree,
Where laughter echoes with such glee.
In a world where quirks are the norm,
The barnyard crew breaks every form.

Requiem for Autumn's Golden Hues

The leaves fell down like little shoes,
Gathering whispers, sharing news.
A pumpkin rolled, it took a trip,
To find a friend and start to skip.

A squirrel chuckled in a haze,
Gathering nuts in a silly maze.
While nearby, a scarecrow grinned,
With a corncob pipe, he looked quite pinned.

The wind uproariously joined the band,
Dancing shadows on the land.
As acorns fell, they had a ball,
While the fog began to softly crawl.

So let's toast to hues so bold,
With tales of laughter to be retold.
In this landscape of vibrant cheer,
Every moment, oh so dear!

Ode to the Gnarled Limbs

The old tree groaned with charm and cheer,
As it hosted branches far and near.
A parrot perched and squawked with flair,
While the woodpecker drummed without a care.

Its twisted trunk held stories spun,
Of rusted nails and raucous fun.
A raccoon peered from a knothole bright,
With wide eyes, filled with mischief and light.

Along came rain, a slippery slide,
As the tree swayed with branches wide.
A family of owls went hooting by,
While a frog leapt up, reaching for the sky.

So here's to the limbs that shake and sway,
In every storm, they find a way.
With laughter echoing in every gust,
In nature's embrace, we all might trust.

Soundscapes of Verdant Realms

In a meadow lush, the grass took flight,
As mice held a party by moonlight.
A badger spun tales, oh so grand,
While fireflies danced, like stars in hand.

The flowers giggled, dressed in hues,
With petals shining, they enjoyed the views.
A rabbit juggled carrots in glee,
While the bees buzzed in perfect harmony.

With each rustle, a secret shared,
In this haven, worries ensnared.
The brook chuckled, tickled by stones,
As the crickets played their rhythmic tones.

Let us wander through laughter's embrace,
In nature's arms, we find our place.
Where joy flows freely, wild and bright,
In this verdant realm, hearts take flight.

Tales of the Weeping Willow

In the park, a tree so round,
With droopy limbs upon the ground.
Squirrels scamper, birds will sing,
'Why so sad?' the children swing.

A raccoon played a prank or two,
Wore a hat, said, 'Look at you!'
The willow sighed, but laughed in time,
'Join my dance, it's quite sublime!'

Underneath, a picnic sprawls,
Food and laughter slowly calls.
Sandwiches fly, juice spills wide,
As the tree joins the joyous ride.

The willow whispered tales from high,
Of flying dreams and clouds that cry.
'Let's all dance,' it then declared,
'If you can't laugh, you must be scared!'

Dream Melodies from the Grove

In twilight, sounds begin to blend,
Crickets chirp, the frogs pretend.
A symphony of silly sights,
With fireflies sparking joyful lights.

A rabbit hops with a twisty dance,
While owls boggle in a trance.
'You can't miss it, come on, folks!'
The forest giggles, the night's in jokes.

Breeze tickles leaves, a cheerful tune,
Giggling shadows under a moon.
'What's that?' a raccoon says with glee,
'It's just the trees having tea with me!'

The night parade is full of cheer,
Each laugh echoes, drawing near.
Join the revel, don't delay,
In dreams, we dance the night away!

Lyricism of Shaded Paths

Down the lane where sunlight dips,
I found a tune that twirls and flips.
A squirrel stomped, the path was wide,
Chased by shadows, oh what a ride!

Leaves chattered secrets overhead,
While wanderers grinned, no one misled.
'What's next?' a sparrow chirped so bright,
'Will we play tag till the morning light?'

The sun, a jester with beams so bold,
Told stories of adventures untold.
With every step, the laughter grew,
Making melodies in shades of blue.

So come and join this winding spree,
Where rhythm lives and spirits flee.
In shadows, we'll find our glow,
As giggles trail, wherever we go!

Hymn of the Sturdy Oaks

Beneath the boughs, a gathering hum,
The sturdy oak has quite the drum.
Its trunk is thick, but don't be fooled,
For underneath, the goofballs ruled.

A crow strutted with a pompous flair,
Declaring wisdom from its lair.
'Adding just a puff of air,
Will keep the world spinning, fair!'

Dancing shadows played peek-a-boo,
While branches flexed as if they knew.
'Why if trees could laugh!' one said,
'We'd tickle gnomes till they fled!'

And so the oaks held a joyous feast,
Where every joke became a beast.
With leaves that clapped, and arms that swayed,
In laughter's grip, we happily stayed!

Harmonizing with the Silent Night

Beneath the moon's bright, winking eye,
A cat sings low, while owls fly high.
Frogs in the pond, they croak a tune,
While fireflies dance, beneath the moon.

A rabbit hops, with shoes too big,
It trips and falls, does a little jig.
The stars all chuckle, light on their feet,
As critters gather for this night's treat.

Squirrels with nuts form a little band,
Play their melodies, it's just so grand!
A raccoon conducts with a twig in paws,
In this wild concert, we can't help but pause.

The night rolls on, a raucous show,
With giggles galore in this midnight glow.
As dawn approaches, we laugh and cheer,
For the funny night, now disappears.

The Whispered Tale of Hidden Gardens

In secret spots, where gnomes might dwell,
The potatoes giggle, oh can't you tell?
Carrots swap stories of what they see,
While radishes cringe at a spider's decree.

Beans sneak around with their stealthy grace,
Hiding from the sun in a leafy embrace.
Cabbages gossip, but no one is near,
In this cracked world, they're the funniest here!

Bees make a buzz, like tiny drums,
Tickling tomatoes, as laughter comes.
In this green circus, oh how they play,
Every root vegetable has something to say.

When the moon rises, they all take flight,
Swinging and swaying, oh what a sight!
With whispers and giggles, the plants intertwine,
In this café of mischief, all's truly divine!

Verses of the Cosmic Cathedral

In a realm above where stars hang low,
Planets play peek-a-boo, putting on a show.
Comets perform, their tails in a twist,
While black holes chuckle at all they've missed.

Aliens dance in their bright neon suits,
With moon cheese hats and cosmic boots.
They spin and they twirl, with joy that ignites,
Painting the heavens with colors so bright.

Saturn grins wide with its rings of flair,
Laughing at Mars with its red, dusty hair.
The Milky Way sings with a voice soft and clear,
Echoing laughter for all stars to hear.

In this celestial circus, who needs gravity?
It's one big party of pure levity.
As nebulas giggle, and quasars delight,
They celebrate life in that faraway light!

Melodies in the Twilight Wood

In the wood, where shadows dance,
A bear does ballet, oh what a chance!
With owls on violins and foxes on drums,
The forest's alive with whimsical hums.

The trees are swaying, a dance-off begins,
As squirrels take bets on who'll score wins.
"Try a backflip!" chirps a chipmunk with glee,
While logs form the stage for a funny spree.

Frogs croak a tune, so offbeat and loud,
As rabbits do stunts, and gather a crowd.
Crickets keep rhythm, with legs all a-twitch,
This twilight assembly is quite the glitch!

As fireflies twirl, igniting the night,
They shimmer and shine with sparkling light.
The wood sings of laughter, mischief, and joy,
In this quirky concert, oh boy, oh boy!

Rooted Rhythms of the Earth

In the garden, worms do dance,
While daisies laugh at their chance.
The sunbeams tickle the grass,
As quirky squirrels strut with sass.

Beneath the oak, a picnic spreads,
With sandwiches, jelly, and some thread.
A bird lands, takes a little bite,
Then flies off like it won a fight.

Frogs in ponds sing out of tune,
While crickets chirp beneath the moon.
Nature's choir, oh what a sight,
With each blunder, pure delight!

A bashful cat climbs up a tree,
And gives a yowl, "Come play with me!"
The bark may creak, but don't you fret,
For laughter's the best safety net!

A Symphony of Scenic Shadows

Underneath the weeping willows,
The shadows dance like bunch of pillows.
Bumblebees wear tiny hats,
While ants in line march like diplomats.

A path that winds, with silly twists,
Where laughter floats like morning mists.
A raccoon tries to steal a bake,
But trips on a branch—Oh for goodness' sake!

Dancing leaves in autumn's breeze,
Perform a jig with effortless ease.
A sneaky worm pops up in style,
And wiggles out with cheeky guile.

In twilight's glow, the frogs applaud,
For nature's antics are never flawed.
In this lush world, with quirks galore,
Who needs a stage? Just open the door!

Verses Along the Woodland Path

A winding path of leafy greens,
Where squirrels wear their acorn jeans.
A deer prances with a wink,
While mushrooms gossip near the sink.

With every step, the stories grow,
Of lost shoes and runaway throws.
A fox in shades, oh what a sight,
Under the disco ball of light.

The breeze hums sweet, a silly tune,
As flowers sway and shake in June.
A butterfly with polka dots,
Shows off its style, connecting lots.

At dusk, the forest takes a bow,
For every mishap we allow.
Life's a jest, both bright and spry,
In woodland paths where giggles fly!

Echoing Through the Arboreal Aisles

In the woods, mischief is afoot,
With creatures wearing mismatched boots.
A crow caws jokes, while pine trees sway,
As laughter carries, come what may.

Beneath the shade, the stories bloom,
Of raccoons in their polka-dot rooms.
A tree stump hosts a gnome with flair,
Who tells tall tales beyond compare.

The wind jokes with twigs on a spree,
Tickling leaves, so wild and free.
A feast of giggles spills on the floor,
As nature's jesters ask for more.

With owls who hoot a silly rhyme,
This lively scene's a playful crime.
In arboreal aisles, joy's the theme,
Where every chuckle's a shared dream!

Poems Carried on the Breeze

In a garden where laughter winks,
Petunias giggle, dandelions think.
A butterfly stumbles in mid-air dance,
As it flirts with a leaf in a frolicsome trance.

Squirrels in suits, they debate the sun,
While ladybugs call it a day, oh what fun!
They slide down the petals, just like on slides,
Upside-down giggles, their humor abides.

A banana peel whispers, "Watch your step!"
As the garden cacti snicker, "Oh, what a rep!"
With roots deep in laughter, they cheer and play,
For every sunbeam holds a joke of the day.

The breeze carries tunes of a comical fate,
Where every leaf rustles with humor innate.
In this bloom of hilarity, we'll end our refrain,
As nature chuckles softly, again and again.

The Soundtrack of Celestial Canopy

Beneath the stars, a raccoon sings,
With a hoot and a holler, it flings.
Owl joins in with a raucous caw,
While moonbeams giggle at the silly draw.

In a chorus of crickets, a sly frog croaks,
With notes that tickle, as everyone pokes.
The wind plays the flute, a whimsical tune,
As fireflies twinkle and dance like a boon.

A funny old tree, it sways cheekily,
Sharing stories of squirrels and their secrecy.
With branches that wave like they're part of the show,
Offering punchlines only the stars know.

As laughter cascades from the heights above,
Every critter beneath feels the warm shove.
In this canopy glitter, under laughter's embrace,
We find ourselves drifting in a jovial space.

Voices from the Undergrowth

In the jungle, a beetle tells jokes with flair,
While ants hold their sides, gasping for air.
A worm wriggles by with a silly grin,
Saying, "Life's a party; come on, jump in!"

A grasshopper breaks into a dance so spry,
Tripping on clovers as time passes by.
Frogs croon a serenade, off pitch, but bold,
With tales of adventures that never grow old.

Snakes slither round, playing games in the shade,
While flowers join in, their laughter displayed.
The mushrooms nod in rhythm, what a sight!
As gossip among ferns spins tales through the night.

With echoes of giggles, the undergrowth roars,
Each critter and plant shares its humorous scores.
In the lively green din, we all find a friend,
For every chuckle in nature has no end.

Stanzas of the Night's Embrace

The moon grins wide with a twinkle in eye,
As shadows play hopscotch and giggle nearby.
Stars sprinkle laughter like confetti on high,
While clouds drift by, dancing just to comply.

A cat in a hat strums a tune on the roof,
Purring along while chasing a poof.
The night's full of antics, a whimsical spree,
With owls hooting sonnets, as lively as glee.

With lanterns aglow, the fireflies boast,
They tell ghostly tales of their ethereal coast.
Each flicker a punchline that flies through the air,
Creating a festival of laughter to share.

As crickets compose in a chorus of cheer,
And sleepy heads bob, it's the laughter we hear.
In the starlit embrace, let our joy take flight,
For the night wraps around us, so cozy and bright.

Lyrical Arches of Nature

In the park, squirrels dare to prance,
While birds above do a silly dance,
A raccoon in a hat strums a tune,
Chasing shadows beneath the moon.

The flowers giggle as the breeze does blow,
Tickling petals, putting on a show,
A butterfly slips, falls in a laugh,
Dancing on air, makes the moment last.

Beneath the tree, whispers of glee,
Each rustle a joke shared merrily,
With branches waving, like hands in delight,
As nature's jesters perform every night.

So join in the fun, take a carefree chance,
Join the woodland zany, come join the dance,
For laughter's the tune that echoes around,
In the heart of the forest, joy can be found.

Refrains of the Rustling Leaves

Leaves chatter softly, sharing their tales,
About a squirrel who lost his way in the trails,
A frog recites rhymes from his prince day,
While crickets add beats to this lively play.

The sun peeks through with a curious gaze,
As bugs tell stories of their summer craze,
A glimmer of mischief in every spark,
As shadows dance freely from dawn until dark.

A twig snaps, and laughter erupts in the air,
A chipmunk declares, "I've got snacks to share!"
Amidst the cacophony, joy takes its flight,
In this leafy realm, everything feels right.

So grab your popcorn, let's hear all the fun,
Nature's comedy show has only begun,
With each rustling leaf, a new plot unfurls,
In the leafy theater, welcome the worlds.

Poetry of the Wandering Roots

Roots twist and turn like a game of charades,
Playing hide and seek beneath the glades,
A wise old tree whispers, "Where's my left foot?"
While a worm jumps up, shouting, "Hey, toot!"

These tangled tales are quite bittersweet,
As vines interlock for a laugh or a cheat,
A beetle spins tales of love in the grass,
While ants carry crumbs, enjoying the sass.

The roots throw a party, a subterranean bash,
With laughter that bubbles, and time that does clash,
Mushrooms narrate the shenanigans deep,
While all the tiny critters begin to creep.

So follow the roots, in this playful sway,
Where the soil sings songs that brighten the day,
For under the surface, the laughter springs free,
In the whimsical world of the wild jubilee.

Echoing Through the Arbor

In the dreamy boughs, echoes bounce off each phase,
A parrot squawks jokes that'll leave you amazed,
As owls in the night roll their big, bright eyes,
And giggle at tales that don't come with lies.

From down in the bushes, a rabbit will chirp,
Sending up laughter, a mad little burp,
The stones on the path chuckle soft with delight,
As shadows engage in a mock moonlit fight.

Each branch holds a tune, a merry refrain,
With rustling and giggling, joy flows like rain,
The trees sway their arms in a wobble and twist,
As they join in the fun to make sure none missed.

So capture the echoes that leap through the green,
With laughter and cheer in this vivid scene,
For in the arbor's embrace, humor can thrive,
In the dance of the forests, we come alive!

Chords of the Gentle Breeze

In a tree with a twist, a squirrel did dance,
He wore tiny shoes, oh what a chance!
With acorns as maracas, he shook with glee,
Singing loud strains to an unbothered bee.

A chorus of crickets joined in the fun,
Each chirp a note, till the day was done.
The sun winked away, stars popped like fizz,
Jolly tunes echoed, oh what a whiz!

A rogue little raccoon stole the stage,
His moonlight antics set off a rage.
Dancing with shadows, oh what a sight,
He juggled with fireflies, sparking delight!

With wind as a friend, laughter did soar,
A symphony built with a whole lot of lore.
As the night rolled in, giggles took flight,
Echoing whispers, a mischievous night.

Harmonies at Dusk's Arrival

As dusk made a show, owls began to hoot,
A concert of sounds, oh, what a hoot!
The frogs croaked a tune in a slippery bog,
While fireflies blinked like a light-up fog.

A rabbit on stage with a top hat sublime,
Recited some verses, but forgot the rhyme!
The crowd of critters chuckled and cheered,
For even in blunders, true joy appeared.

With a breeze in the willows, a flautist afar,
Blew soft melodies, like a wandering star.
A fox spun around, twirling with flair,
His jig left the audience gasping for air!

With each passing moment, the laughter grew wide,
A festival blooming, with cuteness and pride.
As night cloaked the stage, the party did swell,
In the woods under starlight, all under a spell.

Reduced Sonnets of the Sea of Leaves

In an audience of leaves, the whispers arise,
A tree with a grin shared a tale 'neath the skies.
With every soft breeze, giggles would chime,
The sound of short sonnets, oh what a rhyme!

A lizard in a bow tie performed with a flair,
While birds flew in circles, their jokes filled the air.
Crickets took notes with great ardent zeal,
For each tiny stanza spun quite the reel.

The sun creaked in laughter, tickling the earth,
While the roots shared secrets about their great worth.
In this leafy expanse, they created a ball,
Fables and riddles spun out for them all.

With every soft rustle, a giggle set free,
They crafted their moments with utmost glee.
Sonnets reduced, yet the spirit did soar,
In the vast sea of leaves, who could ask for more?

The Secret Song of Hollow Trunks

In hollowed-out trunks, secrets did dwell,
A woodpecker knocked like he was ringing a bell.
With laughter and rhythm, he startled a snail,
Who stretched out her neck with a wobbly trail.

A party ensued, where moss wore a crown,
A bash of the sprites, all frolicked around.
"Join in!" sang the mushrooms, with caps oh so bright,
As shadows choreographed wild dances at night.

The secretive whispers from the bark did resound,
Echoes of chuckles from the creatures around.
As the owls lent their eyes, the moon scribbled light,
The trunks held their secrets, toning hilarity's flight.

With each playful rustle, the stories took shape,
Of critters and giggles in their bark-turned-ape.
A ballad of laughter, they rolled and they spun,
In hollowed-out trunks, where the fun's never done.

A Canticle Beneath the Stars

In the glow of night, a squirrel did prance,
He thought he could sing, but forgot the dance.
With a jump and a twist, he tripped on his tail,
A concert of giggles, his grand face turned pale.

An owl gave a hoot, a hearty chortle,
While the crickets played on, not missing the mortal.
A frog joined the chorus, croaking with zeal,
In this wild night's tune, no serious deal!

The stars all aligned for an evening escape,
While a fox in a tux tried to juggle some grapes.
With a slip and a flop, he fell in a bush,
And giggling galore was the resultant rush!

So beneath twinkling lights, the creatures did sway,
In a harmony crafted from playful dismay.
A silly old choir, no fear in the air,
Just laughter and joy, and a wiggle to share.

The Ballad of Seasons Past

In the autumn, the leaves were a fluttery show,
While the wind made a mess of a grand fashion row.
Accident-prone kids, in piles they would land,
Claiming victory loud as the leaves made a stand.

Winter crept in with a snowman's delight,
Alas, a dread snowball. Oh, what a fright!
With a flurry of fun, they called for a fight,
Now their mittens were soaked, but their spirits were bright.

Come spring, the frogs croaked a comical tune,
Whilst the flowers all giggled beneath a full moon.
A bee buzzing near, thought he'd play the star,
But slipped on a petal and skidded quite far!

Then summer arrived, with a barbecue flare,
Where the burgers exploded and made quite a scare.
As they chomped down the bites, they laughed until sore,
Ah, the seasons rolled on, with tales to explore!

Rhythms of the Quiet Meadow

In the meadow so green, a rabbit took note,
Of the songs sung by bees, and a pig in a coat.
With a wiggle and jiggle, the grass danced in glee,
While the daisies debated how tall they could be.

A butterfly waltzed, but a gust caused alarm,
As she tumbled and swirled, losing all of her charm.
She stuck to a thistle, a dizzy surprise,
And the daisies just giggled, with sparkles in eyes.

The frogs on a lily, in circles they spun,
Croaked a funny duet, laughing even more fun.
A turtle then joined in, moving oh-so-slow,
Made a grand entrance, just to steal the show!

So in this bright meadow, the antics unfold,
With laughter and chatter, and stories retold.
Each creature a player in this joyful play,
A rhythm of fun that won't soon fade away.

Poetry of the Lush Greenways

In the lush of the green, where mischief runs free,
A raccoon wore shades, thought he handsome would be.
With a strut and a grin, he stole snacks from the crew,
They chased him in giggles, oh, what a hullabaloo!

The hedgehogs rolled by, oh what a hard race,
They wobbled and tumbled, it was all over the place.
With laughter erupting, they just couldn't cope,
As they zigzagged around their own spiky slope.

A bird then flew in, with a joke on her beak,
"Told my mate he should learn to dance, what a geek!"
So the trees all chuckled, leaves rattled in cheer,
As the adventures ensued, under skies so clear.

Thus in the greenways, where laughter is found,
The critters all gather, such joy does abound.
A portrait of whimsy, penned with each cheer,
In the poetry of life, let's spread it right here!

Melodies Woven in the Mist

In the fog, a crow did croon,
Twirling leaves like a cartoon.
Squirrels danced upon the ground,
Dropping acorns all around.

Mice in tuxedos, oh so neat,
Tapping toes to the rhythm of feet.
A rabbit played a tambourine,
While frogs performed, oh what a scene!

The breeze whistled a silly tune,
While owls hooted by the moon.
Every branch swayed to the beat,
As nature's choir made it sweet.

With laughter ringing through the air,
A concert held without a care.
In this misty, joyful place,
The world spun with a giggly grace.

Resounding Through the Thicket

In a thicket, sly fox sang,
Winging it with every twang.
Bunnies hopping to the tune,
Joining in from noon till moon.

Petty thieves, the raccoons laugh,
Stealing snacks, they cut in half.
The woodpecker joined the fray,
Pecking beats in a playful way.

Branches sway both left and right,
Tickling leaves in pure delight.
A jolly dance, the critters prance,
In sunshine's glow, they take a chance.

The thicket rang with joy so bright,
A bustling stage of pure delight.
With every note, the giggles grew,
As laughter echoed, wild and true.

Tales in the Timberline

Under the pines, the stories flow,
From a turtle who claimed he could glow.
A parrot shared tales of grandeur,
Of pirate ships and treasure sure.

Beneath a big hat, the raccoon sat,
Spinning yarns with a grin like a cat.
The deer stood by, rolling their eyes,
As squirrels threw in their own surprise.

Frogs croaked out a dramatic scene,
While chipmunks giggled, keeping it clean.
Each tale a twist, a silly tale,
Of speaking trees and a wallaby's sail.

And as the sun dipped low that day,
The laughter carried, come what may.
Every critter, it seemed so free,
In woodland tales, we find our glee.

Echoes of the Rooted Adventure

Deep in the woods, a squirrel spun,
A tale of glory, oh what fun!
He claimed to be the king of trees,
With acorns flying like summer breeze.

The forest echoed, giggles loud,
As chipmunks cheered, all so proud.
A fox in boots waved from afar,
Sipping cider, a woodland star.

A bear in shades, so cool he seemed,
Snoring loud while the whole crew dreamed.
The stars above joined in the jest,
Casting beams of laughter best.

In every nook of nature's spree,
Adventures thrived, wild and free.
With every rustle, a cheerful cheer,
In rooted fun, the joy was clear.

www.ingramcontent.com/pod-product-compliance
Lightning Source LLC
Chambersburg PA
CBHW072214070526
44585CB00015B/1339